Bodies [storytime kit]
Total - 22 pieces

You Have Healthy Bones!

By Susan DerKazarian

Consultant
Nanci R. Vargus, Ed.D.
Assistant Professor of Literacy
University of Indianapolis, Indianapolis, Indiana

Children's Press®
A Division of Scholastic Inc.
New York Toronto London Auckland Sydney
Mexico City New Delhi Hong Kong
Danbury, Connecticut

Designer: Herman Adler Design
Photo Researcher: Caroline Anderson
The photo on the cover shows a boy with healthy bones.

Library of Congress Cataloging-in-Publication Data

Derkazarian, Susan, 1969-
You have healthy bones! / by Susan Derkazarian.
p. cm. — (Rookie read-about health)
Includes index.
ISBN 0-516-25878-8 (lib. bdg.) 0-516-27919-X (pbk.)
1. Bones—Juvenile literature. I. Title. II. Series.
QM101.D47 2005
611'.71—dc22

2004015307

1 2 3 4 5 6 7 8 9 10 R 14 13 12 11 10 09 08 07 06 05

You have hundreds of bones in your body!

A newborn baby has more than 300 bones.

As you grow, some bones join together. An adult has 206 bones.

Bones grow and change as you get older. They are alive like the rest of your body.

Bones even have blood in them! There are red blood cells and white blood cells.

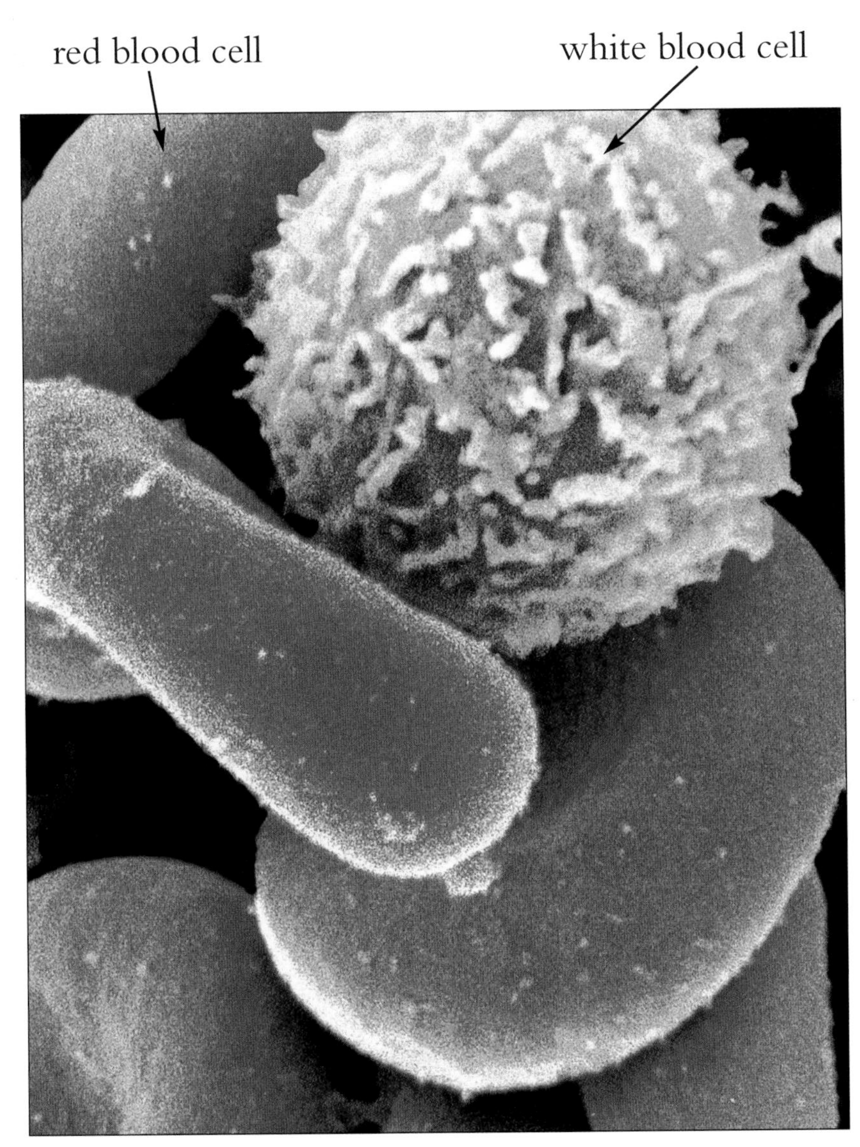

This is what your blood looks like through a microscope.

This girl can jump rope because her bones are healthy.

Bones help you stand up, jump, and walk around.

You need bones to do almost everything!

Different bones do
different things.

The bones in your legs
help you stand up.

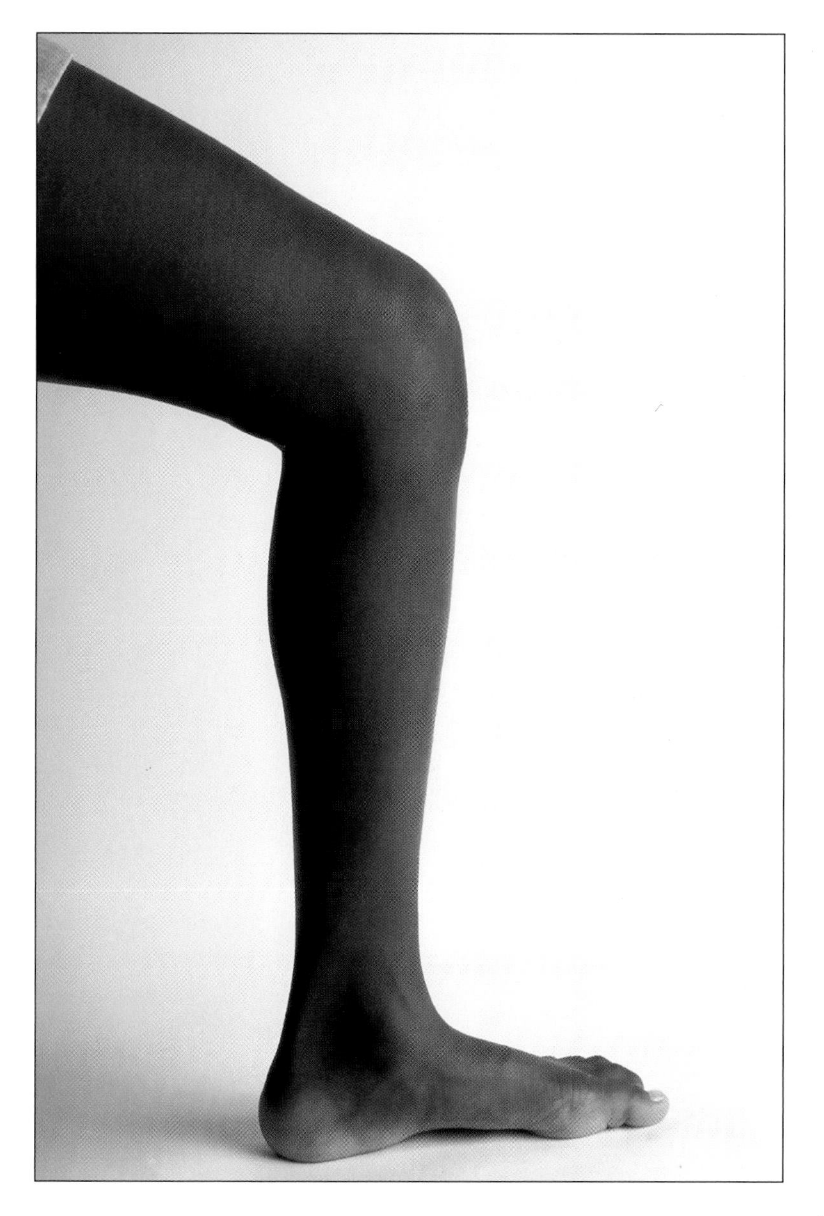

Other bones cover the
organs inside your body.

Your ribs cover your heart,
lungs, and other organs.

All of your bones are very important. Visit the doctor to make sure your bones are healthy.

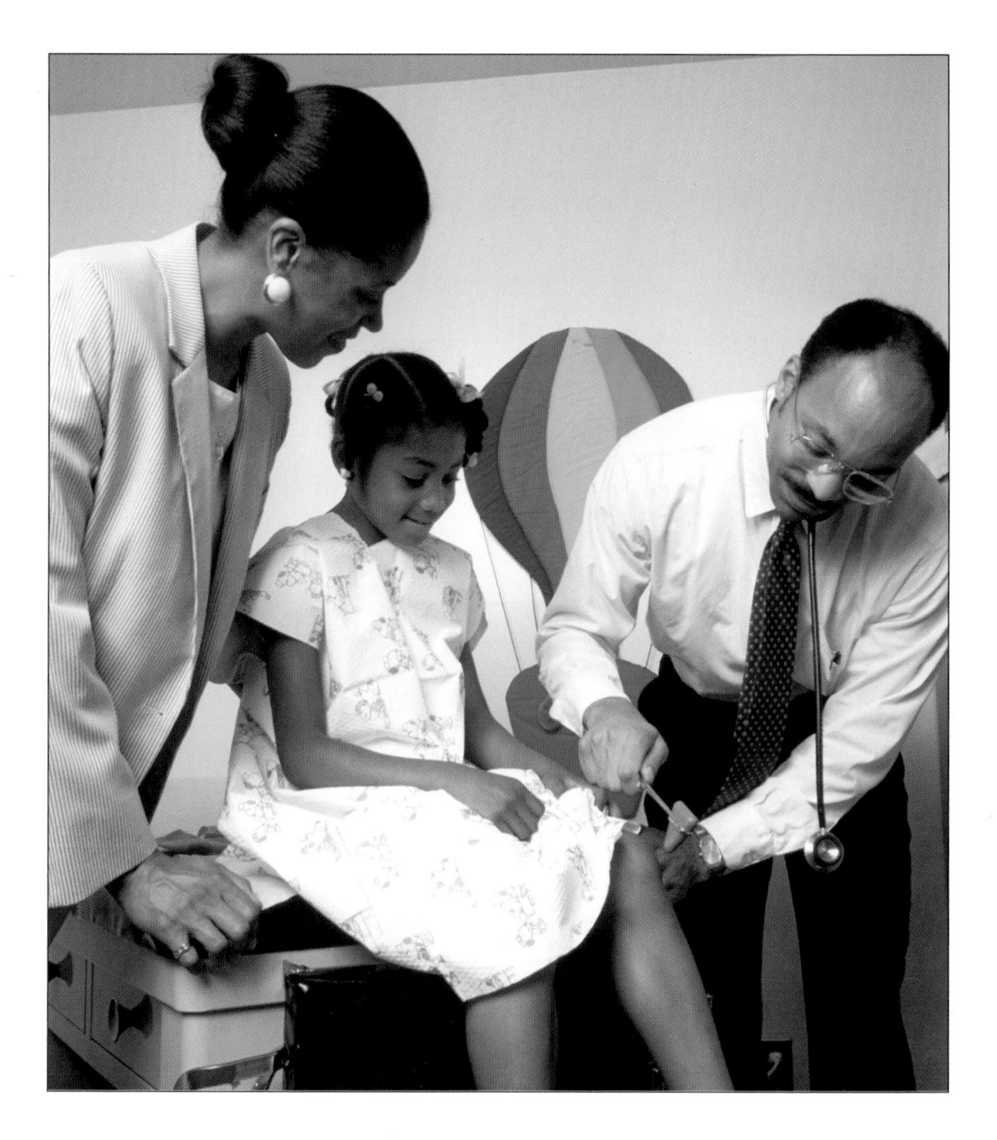

Drinking milk can keep your bones healthy, too.

Milk has calcium in it. Calcium helps your bones become strong and hard.

Exercise is another way
to keep your bones healthy.

Playing soccer is good
exercise.

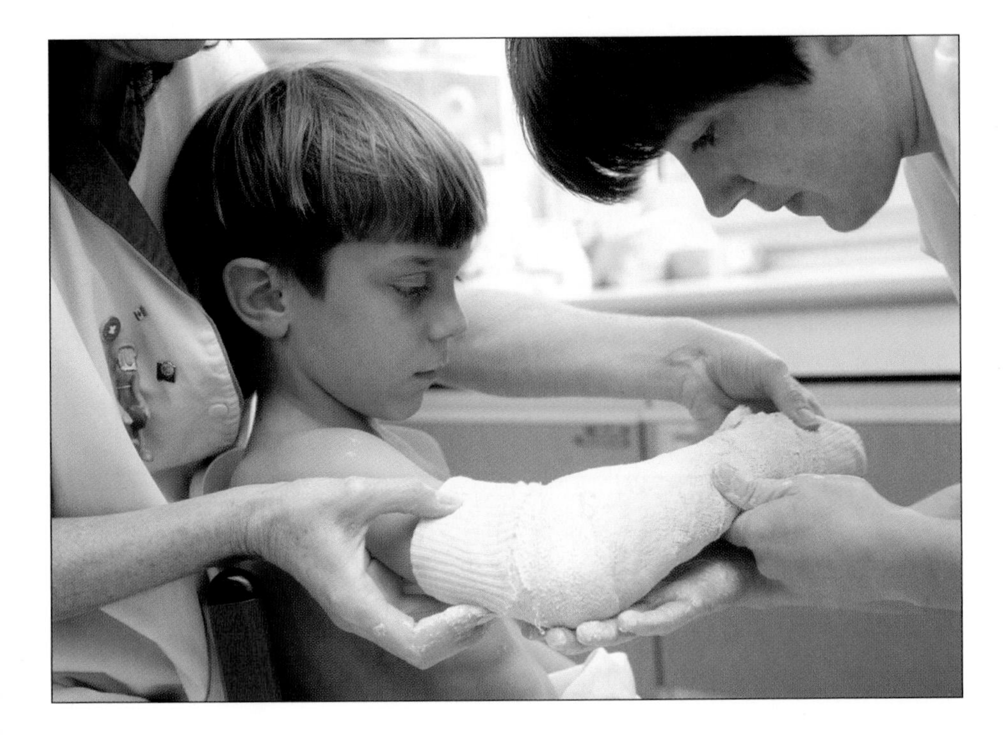

Breaking a bone hurts.
It can be scary.

If you break a bone, you
will need a cast. The cast
lets the bone heal.

You can protect your bones.

Be careful when you play. Do not jump from high places.

Are these kids playing safely?

ROSS

Always wear a helmet when you ride your bicycle.

A helmet will protect the bones in your head. These bones are your skull. Your skull protects your brain.

Wear pads on your knees and elbows when you skate.

If you fall, you might land hard. The bones in your knee or elbow might break.

Take care of your bones, and your bones will take care of you!

Words You Know

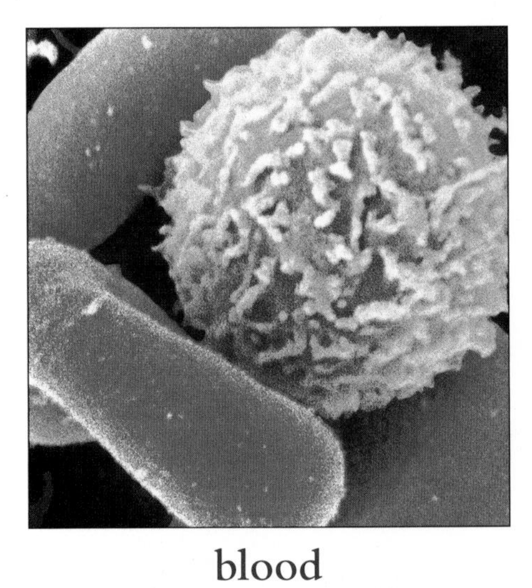

blood

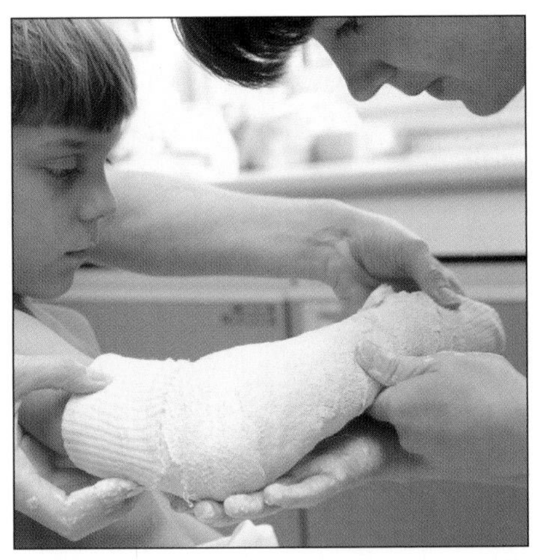

cast

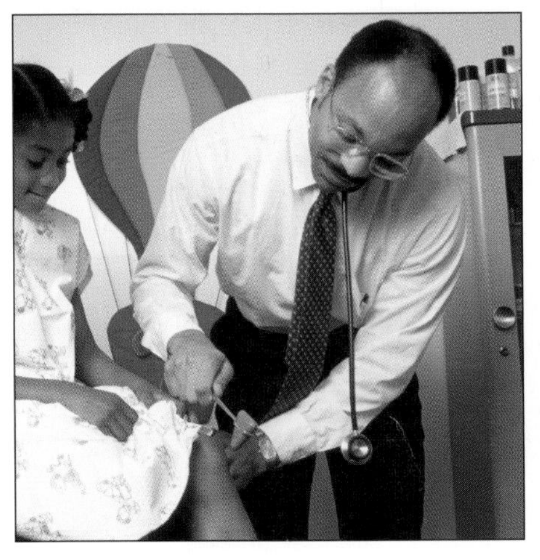

doctor

exercise

helmet

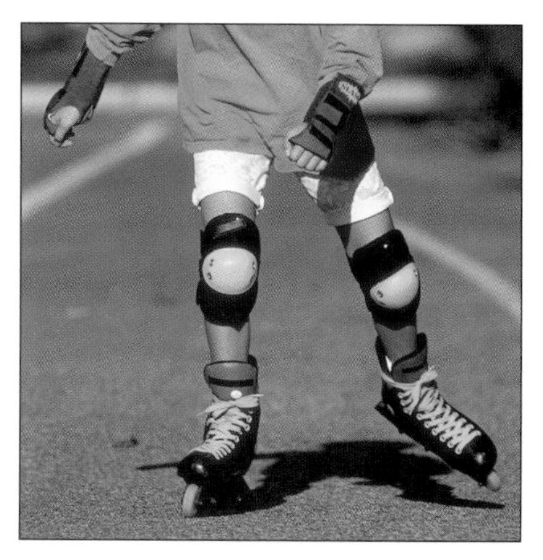

knee pads

milk

Index

About the Author

Susan DerKazarian is a senior editor at a publishing company in New York City. She also writes many science books for kids. Her favorite things to do are reading, going to the beach, and hiking.

Photo Credits

Photographs © 2005: Photo Researchers, NY: 24, 31 top left (bachmann), 16, 31 bottom (Oscar Burriel/SPL), 8, 27, 31 top right (Tim Davis), 20, 30 top right (Garo), 4 (Margaret Miller), 19, 30 bottom right (Rita Nannini), 15, 30 bottom left (Blair Seitz); PhotoEdit: 3, 11 (Spencer Grant), 29 (Jeff Greenberg), cover, 23 (Richard Hutchings), 12 (Michael Newman); Stone/Getty Images/Yorgos Nikas: 7, 30 top left.